AT ALL TIMES

AND IN ALL PLACES

The Choir
Basilica of S. Clemente, Rome

AT ALL TIMES
AND
IN ALL PLACES

THIRD EDITION, REVISED

Massey H. Shepherd, Jr.

The Seabury Press • New York

ACKNOWLEDGMENTS

The author wishes to express his thanks to The Macmillan Company for permission to quote from William Temple, *The Hope of a New World* (New York, 1941), in Chapter VI.

For assistance in assembling the illustrations, he is grateful to the staff of the William Hayes Fogg Art Museum of Harvard University; and (for Plate IX) to the Rev. James Roberton MacColl, III, and the Rev. Peter Chase of Trinity Church, Newport, Rhode Island; and (for Plate XI) to Kent School, Kent, Connecticut; and (for Plate XII) to Grace Church, Madison, Wisconsin; and (for Plate X) to Miss Grace A. Littell of the Diocesan Library, Diocese of Massachusetts, Boston.

Acknowledgment is also gratefully made for permissions to reproduce the following illustrations: The Frontispiece, to D. Anderson, Rome; Plate III, to Fratelli Alinari, Florence; Plate IV, to the Dumbarton Oaks Research Library and Collection, Harvard University; Plate V, to the Trustees of the British Museum; Plate VI, to the Pierpont Morgan Library, New York.

TO

SAINT JOHN'S PARISH

ROXBURY

PREFACE

The six chapters in this book are sketches depicting typical scenes of the celebration of the Holy Communion in different periods of Christian history. Each period has impressed upon the rite its own special emphasis and meaning, its own taste in ceremonial and artistic adornment. Yet the service remains throughout the ages essentially the same as that which the apostles received from the Lord Jesus at the Last Supper. It is this unity of spirit amidst the diversity of gifts—"at all times and in all places"—that constitutes the theme of this book. For the reader who will take his place with sympathy and imagination among the worshippers in these several services, it is hoped that he will find his own participation in our glorious heritage of Common Prayer enlarged and enriched in meaning, and his consciousness of his place in the communion of saints deepened and broadened in perspective.

The periods and places chosen for description are as follows: 1) A celebration of the Eucharist in one of the house-churches that might be found in almost any city of the Roman Empire during the time that the Church was persecuted and many of its members won the crown of martyrdom. 2) The Liturgy in a basilican church of a city of Western Europe at the time when the Roman world was breaking up amidst the inroads and settlements of the Germanic barbarians—the type of liturgy that St. Augustine and his fellow Benedictine monks brought with them on their mission to the English people at the close of the sixth century. 3) The Sunday Mass of an English village's parish church in the late Middle Ages, just prior to the Reformation of the Church, which began under King Henry VIII, a service that formed the basis for the reformed rite in the Book of Common Prayer. 4) The Easter service of an English parish shortly after the Restoration of King Charles II, such as was observed also in Anglican churches of the American colonies. 5) Divine service in a parish of the Protestant Episcopal Church in the early part of the nineteenth century, before the revival known as the Oxford Movement. 6) The Holy Communion in an Episcopal parish *of the future*, located in an industrial community.

A word of explanation about this last chapter is necessary. No attempt has been made in this sketch to suggest a revision of the liturgy as it now stands in our Prayer Book or to indulge in descriptions of ceremonial that are occasion of controversy. Rather, the aim has been to portray the Church's living worship in the modern world, inspired and illuminated by the ideals of the contemporary liturgical revival now going on throughout Christendom, a movement in which our Anglican Communion has made, and will continue to make, a large and wholesome contribution.

This book was first published in 1947 as the Lenten booklet of the Church Congress in the United States. A continuing demand for it has led to the present new edition, enlarged by the addition of Chapter IV and the illustrations. The bibliography has also been revised and augmented for those who wish to study the sources and references upon which the several chapters are based.

CONTENTS AND PLATES

ONE

HEIRS OF THE

EVERLASTING KINGDOM

A.D. 150

The faintest glimmer of dawn was edging above the
eastern horizon when the slave Felix knocked softly at
the street door of a small stucco house. With him was
the slender, delicate, fifteen year old child of his master,
Dorothea, who had been baptized only a week before at
the *Pascha*, the Easter celebration. Her mother, the lady
Marcia, usually accompanied the two, but this Sunday
she was not well enough to come. For many years Marcia
had hoped to offer her spacious town house for the worship of the Christians, but her husband, a staunch pagan,
refused to permit his premises to be used by the raga-
muffin devotees to whom she had become stubbornly
attached—most of them slaves or small-tradesmen. It was
a source of anxious grief to him that his wife had fallen
a victim to this debased superstition which had arisen
among the Jews, and about which there were current
many scandalous, indecent tales concerning their secret
rites. Yet he had no certain knowledge of these things,

and the behavior of his wife in the home gave him no indication of any impropriety on her part. He was inclined to trust her word that the cult of the Christians was innocent of any vicious practice, and he agreed to keep his lips guarded on the subject of her religion. None the less he was haunted by an inward fear lest the honor of his name and house be smirched should she ever be apprehended by the police.

At Felix's knock a porter noiselessly opened the door, and when he recognized the pair let them in. Through a narrow vestibule they passed to a colonnaded court or *atrium*, in the center of which was a shallow pool. About the court the catechumens, who were still receiving instruction and undergoing a period of testing before they could be qualified to receive baptism, were standing. With them were a few interested strangers, friends of some of the church members. These had been admitted to the house upon guarantee that they would neither betray the place of meeting nor the names of the Christians to the magistrates. Dorothea no longer had to take her place among them, but passed on to the farther side of the court where the faithful were gathering, including the friends who had received baptism with her the week before, all of whom were still wearing the new white linen garments given them after the bath of the baptismal water. These garments symbolized the clean, new life into which they had entered—hence their name of *candidates*, a word meaning "robed in white."

Felix meanwhile repaired to one of the side rooms off the *atrium* to fetch the parchment books of the Scriptures which he was to read at the service. Many of these books he had copied himself, for he was a skillful scribe.

For several years now he had been the official *reader* of the church, but he hoped soon to be ordained a deacon. His business ability and experience gained through his work for his master would be of great help to the bishop in the management of the financial affairs of the church.

When he returned to the court with the books, the deacons were lighting the pendant terra cotta lamps about the interior of the house. Their soft, flickering light revealed the arrangement and furnishing of the place. Opening off the court on three sides were rooms of various size, one a baptistery, others used as class rooms for the catechist, storerooms, offices, and guestchambers for any traveling Christians who needed accommodations on their journey. The far end of the court, where the faithful were gathering—the men on one side, the women on the other—opened full length into a large dining hall. In the center of the room stood a small table. To the right, where the room and court joined, was a platform with a reading stand and large lamp. Felix placed his books here.

There was little other furniture. A few small benches or falstools were provided for some of the older women. Behind the table was a semicircular row of seven seats where the presbyters of the church were gathered. Most of these men were of advanced age and had served long in the faith. Two of them bore scars from tortures they had endured in prison. The center seat among them, directly facing the people—and the only real chair, since it had a back—was reserved for the bishop.

Decorations were in keeping with the simplicity of the furnishing. The floor was paved with a marble mosaic of geometric patterns enclosed by a conventional border design of vines and pomegranates with birds and winged cupids fluttering among the branches. This mosaic antedated the time the Christians acquired the house, and it had been skillfully executed by pagan craftsmen. The Christians, however, had left it as it was, and read into the border design a symbolic representation of the blissful life of the redeemed in paradise. On the walls of the court, between the doors of the rooms, were several frescoes painted by amateur Christian hands. They included scenes of the Good Shepherd (depicted as a smooth-shaven youth), the raising of Lazarus, Daniel between two lions, the healing of the paralytic in the pool of Bethesda, and a group of bread baskets and fishes recalling the miracle of the feeding of the five thousand. In the quiet light and shadows these crude pictures suggested a faith and hope and endurance beyond the power of any human hand to draw—the mighty acts of deliverance of a loving and compassionate Saviour.

The congregation gathered before the table was composed chiefly of working folk of the lower classes. The apostle would have recognized them as the "not many wise, not many mighty, not many noble" of his own mission churches. They were dressed in sleeved, knee-length linen tunics, girded about the waist. Over the tunics, for protection from the damp chill of the morning air, they wore a woolen cloak, the *paenula* or chasuble. This was a round piece of cloth through which the head passed by a hole in the middle and which then fell over the arms and draped the body down to the knees. Instead of the *paenula* several of the men, including two of the presbyters and many of the women, wore the *pallium*, a long rectangular piece of wool wrapped crosswise around the body and fastened with a pin over the left shoulder. The women covered their heads with a veil or hood-shaped fold of the *pallium*. The deacons, who had taken their places standing on either side of the table, facing the people, wore only their girded tunics. Across the left arm they had a folded towel or napkin (the *maniple* of later times) which they would need for their ministrations.

PLATE I

The Eucharist

Catacomb of Callistus, Rome

A grave silence in the room was punctuated occasionally by a fervent *Alleluia* or a *Kyrie eleison* ("Lord, have mercy"). Presently from the rear of the house an aged gentleman entered, clad in tunic and *pallium* with a scarf about his neck. It was Bishop Postumus. He greeted his flock with the ancient salutation: "The Lord be with you," to which all replied: "And with thy spirit." Then taking his seat with the presbyters, he motioned to Felix to begin the reading.

Felix mounted the platform where the lectern stood and announced a lesson from the prophet Isaiah:

> Awake, awake, put on strength,
>   O arm of the Lord;
> Awake, as in the ancient days,
>   in the generations of old.

> Art thou not it which hath dried the sea,
>   the waters of the great deep;
> That hath made the depths of the sea a way
>   for the ransomed to pass over?

> Therefore the redeemed of the Lord shall return,
>   and come with singing unto Zion:
> And everlasting joy shall be upon their head:
>   they shall obtain gladness and joy;
>   and sorrow and mourning shall flee away.

At a signal from the bishop, Felix ended the reading and stepped down from the platform. One of the deacons took his place and began to chant with simple cadences the ancient psalm of the Passover:

> When Israel came out of Egypt,
>   and the house of Jacob from among the
>   strange people. . . .

The people joined in a refrain of *Alleluia* at the end. A second and a third lesson followed. Felix read first from the Epistle of Peter; then from the Gospel of John the account of the Lord's appearance to Thomas after His resurrection from the dead.

Bishop Postumus, seated in his chair, addressed his flock. He spoke first of the joy of the whole church in the new members who had been received by baptism the previous week, and called their attention to the words of

PLATE II

Mosaic Pavement
Basilica of Theodore, Aquileia

· 17 ·

the apostle which had just been read: "Be ready always to give an answer to every man that asketh you a reason for the hope that is in you." He reminded them of the danger and afflictions which threatened them, and reviewed the company of witnesses into whose fellowship they had entered, especially the great apostle himself. He told them how as a boy he had known one of Peter's disciples, and how from his lips he had heard an account of the glorious confession that disciple made in the persecution of Nero. The bishop then went on to exhort the older members to pattern their lives after Christ and set an example for the new members. He closed by recalling how long he had tried to teach them, saying that his end was near at any time, and urging them to keep undefiled the deposit of faith which had been committed to them.

The bishop's homily ended—the sad note of what seemed a farewell, leaving a momentary pause of silence —the deacons addressed themselves to the catechumens out in the court:

O catechumens, bow your heads for a blessing.

When the bishop had given them a blessing, the deacons took up again:

Let the catechumens depart!

Let no unbaptized person remain!

Quietly the group of catechumens and pagan visitors were shown to the door by the porter. Assured that all had left, he secured the door against any intrusion, though he remained standing near enough to the entrance to be ready for any emergency should the faithful need warning of imminent danger.

The assembled company fell to prayer. The bishop would bid the prayers—for the whole Church throughout the world, for the Emperor and the peace and security of his dominion, for the sick and those in affliction, especially those in prison "for the Name," for travelers and sojourners and the unconverted, and for the faithful departed in Christ. After each bidding all prayed silently for a space on their knees. Then the deacons bade them rise, and the bishop summed up the intercessions in a brief "collect" expressive of the intentions of them all.

Now the bishop summoned all to the holy kiss of peace, himself beginning by exchanging the kiss with the presbyters. They in turn kissed the deacons. Among the laity the men kissed the men and the women the women. By this simple apostolic ceremony—the occasion, alas, of so much ill gossip among outsiders—they expressed the unity and godly love of all the members of God's holy family in Christ Jesus. All were now ready for the holy sacrifice.

The deacons spread a linen cloth over the table and set upon it a silver platter and a two-handled cup. The people formed in line to bring to the table their bread and wine, for each one had brought his own offering, a small bun and a tiny flask of wine. One deacon received the loaves in a wicker basket, the other held a large *amphora* into which each poured the wine from his flask. Likewise the bishop and presbyters made their offering. When all the wine and loaves were gathered, the deacons presented them to the bishop, who selected as much bread as was needed for the communion and filled the smaller chalice from the larger. The remaining offerings were set at the side of the table, and the deacons retook their customary stand on either side facing the people.

With his presbyters gathered about him the bishop

· 19 ·

now began to intone the thanksgiving, bidding the people:

Sursum corda! Lift up your hearts!

The responses of the people given, the bishop and presbyters laid their hands upon the oblation of the holy food while the bishop continued his solemn chant:

> We give thanks unto thee, O Lord God, who art worthy of praise from every creature, whom thou hast made, and whom thou dost ever sustain and nourish by thy grace; because in these last days thou hast sent thine only Son to be a Saviour and Redeemer of mankind, to bring us out of darkness into light, out of error into truth, out of death into life; and hast forgiven our sins, and illumined our minds, and made us worthy to stand before thee. . . .

Here the bishop proceeded to recite the traditional account of the Last Supper, the Lord's words of institution, then he continued:

> We therefore offer unto thee this bread for the refreshing of our souls, and this cup of everlasting salvation, making remembrance of his death and resurrection, and giving thanks unto thee. And we beseech thee to send thy Holy Spirit upon this oblation, and upon thy Church, that he may fill us and unite us in thy kingdom. To thee be praise and honor and worship through Jesus Christ thy Son, with Holy Spirit in holy Church unto the ages of ages.

And all shouted *Amen*. A brief blessing of the extra bread and wine was made. Whereupon the bishop broke before the people one of the consecrated loaves on the holy table, and communicated himself and his presbyters; and each of them sipped from the cup. Now the people came forward, and the bishop placed a piece of bread in the hand of each one, saying:

The Bread of Heaven in Christ Jesus.

One of the deacons held the cup. Each one drank of it, and said *Amen*. When all had been communicated, the deacons gave a nod to the people to come forward again with their little boxes to receive some of the remaining holy bread to take home. The deacons also took some of it to carry to the sick and absent immediately after the dismissal—which they announced, as soon as the vessels were cleansed, with the brief phrase: "Go in peace."

Silently the faithful dispersed, each upon his own way. Felix and Dorothea remained a moment to await the deacon who would accompany them home to communicate Dorothea's mother. Felix wished also to speak with the bishop about his coming ordination. But suddenly there appeared in the room, as if from nowhere, a magistrate and three soldiers.

"Are you Christians?" asked the magistrate.

"We are," they replied. . . .

In the register of the church this entry was made:

On the day before the Kalends of May: Postumus, the bishop; Marcus, the deacon; Felix, the reader; and Dorothea. *Birthday in eternity!*

TWO

THESE HOLY MYSTERIES

A.D. 500

Timothy hurriedly closed his law books to join the throng coming in procession down the street. The entire populace seemed to be turning out in honor of St. Stephen the protomartyr, exemplar of all believers who had followed their Lord in a baptism of blood. Edging his way into the crowd about the procession, Timothy joined the chorus as they half-chanted, half-shouted their acclamations:

> Hear us, O Christ!
> Long life to our Bishop!
> St. Stephen, help us!
> *Kyrie eleison!*

At the head of the procession acolytes carried tapers. Behind them came the deacons and subdeacons, one of them holding the Gospel book. The chancellor of the diocese and other lay councilors and officials followed on horseback. Bishop Gregory also rode astride a finely caparisoned horse. Before him went a deacon bearing incense. Grooms attended him on either side. Such honor had of old been accorded in public processions only to the Emperor or to the highest magistrates who were his deputies. But in these troublous times the lights of eternal

Rome's wide dominion were growing dim in the Western world. For most communities the bishops had become in fact the governors and defenders of the people. At the rear of the procession, on foot behind the bishop, were the officers of his household and acolytes who carried the sacred vessels and ornaments for the Eucharist. The deacons and the bishop were vested in the ancient Roman dress with tunics, dalmatics, and chasubles. But the bishop was distinguished by a white woolen scarf or *pall*, which fell in deep curved lines from the shoulders both in front and in back—another ensign of high rank borrowed from the ceremonial of the State.

When the bishop and his party arrived at the basilica where the Eucharist was to be celebrated this day, he was greeted at the entrance by the presbyters who served the church and by the local lay officials. He blessed them, then repaired to the sacristy near the door for the final preparations for the service. Timothy and his fellow worshippers passed on into the open, colonnaded court with its bubbling fountain that stood before the basilica proper. The portico on the far side of the court served also as a narthex. As Timothy stepped beneath its wide arches to go into the body of the church, he observed the catechumens and penitents standing there. They were not permitted to worship with the faithful: the catechumens because they were as yet unbaptized, the penitents because they were undergoing temporary discipline and excommunication for certain grievous offenses. They could, however, see and hear the service through the great doors that separated the narthex from the main body of the interior—at least until such time as they would be dismissed.

The main body of the basilica was a long, rectangular hall called the *nave*, a word meaning "ship," for the Church was likened to the Ark of Noah, a place of refuge and deliverance from the troublous, destructive waves of the world. Broad aisles flanked the entire length of the nave on either side and made it easy to enter or leave the service with a minimum of disturbance. Through the windows in the clerestory, which rose above the colonnaded arches separating nave and aisles, the clear light was tempered and set aglow from the varicolored mosaics of Biblical scenes set in the spaces between. On the north side were portrayed mystic types of the Eucharist from both Old and New Testaments— Abel's sacrifice of his firstlings, Abraham ready to offer his only son Isaac, and Melchizedek, King of Salem and "Priest of the Most High God," bringing forth bread and wine to refresh Abraham and to bless him:

> Blessed be Abram of the most high God,
> possessor of heaven and earth:
> And blessed be the most high God,
> who hath delivered thine enemies
> into thy hand.

Gospel scenes included the miracle of the loaves and fishes, and the wedding feast at Cana when the Lord changed water into wine.

Between the windows on the south side was the story of the Passion and Resurrection, beginning with the Last Supper and ending triumphantly in the disciples' "joy when they saw the Lord" as He showed them His hands and side, saying:

> Peace be unto you.
> Receive ye the Holy Ghost.

PLATE III

Old Testament Types of the Eucharist
Basilica of S. Apollinare in Classe, Ravenna

(Alinari)

Timothy was always fascinated by these pictures. When-
ever his eye scanned them, he felt that he too was being
carried in procession down that *via crucis* and up Calvary,
and on beyond it to the divine denouement of the drama.
Finally, his eye would come to rest on the great mosaic
in the curving arch of the apse, which looked out over
the holy Table and its protecting baldachin, centered on
the chord of the apse. It was a majestic, full-face picture
of Christ the Judge of the quick and the dead, throned
upon the orb of the world, holding in his left hand the
"book sealed with seven seals" of the Apocalypse. Approaching him were four figures, two on either side—on
the right, the chief apostles, St. Peter and St. Paul; on the
left, St. Stephen and the Bishop Eusebius who had erected
the basilica to enshrine the relics of the martyr. The face
of the Christ held Timothy's attention fast. How awesome
in majesty, glorious in appearing! And Timothy bowed
his head and repeated in tremulous excitement:

> *Kyrie eleison, Kyrie eleison!*
> Lord, have mercy; Lord, have mercy!

When he looked up, he saw one of the deacons with
the Gospel book advancing down the nave to the altar.
The liturgy was about to begin. Timothy looked towards
the choir of men and boys who stood within the low
screen or chancel extending out from the apse about a
third of the way into the nave. They had started the
Introit, the psalm-chant sung to accompany the bishop's
solemn entry into the church. Today its verses were taken
from the 119th Psalm:

ANTIPHON

> Princes did sit and speak against me,
> the wicked persecuted me falsely.

O be thou my help, O Lord, my God,
  for thy servant is occupied in thy statutes.

PSALM

Blessed are those that are undefiled in the way,
  and walk in the law of the Lord.
Blessed are they that keep his testimonies,
  and seek him with their whole heart.

PLATE IV

Communion of the Apostles
Silver Paten from Riha on the Orontes, Syria

(Courtesy of the Dumbarton Oaks Research Library and Collection, Harvard University)

Timothy recognized these verses. They were often sung at the feasts of the martyrs. While the choir continued, interpolating the antiphon between the psalm verses, the bishop, escorted by his deacons and acolytes, with their tapers and incense, proceeded down the nave amongst the people into the chancel where the choir was singing. On his approach the presbyters left their seats in the apse and descended the steps on either side of the altar to meet him in the chancel. Bishop Gregory gave them the kiss of peace, after which the presbyters with the deacons escorted him to his throne at the back of the apse, directly facing the people, while the choir started the *Gloria Patri* of the psalm.

Thus the household of God, each in his own order, arranged themselves for the holy mysteries. When the choir finished singing, there was a moment of silence, tense, expectant, as all awaited the bishop's simple greeting: "The Lord be with you." The whole basilica gave back, as with one voice, the response: "And with thy spirit." "Let us pray," said the bishop, and he intoned the Collect of the day:

> Almighty and everlasting God, grant to us, we beseech thee, to imitate that which we cherish; that we may learn to love our enemies, even as thy martyr Stephen, who prayed for his persecutors to thy Son, our Lord Jesus Christ, who livest and reignest with thee and the Holy Spirit, one God, world without end.

The people's *Amen* resounded through the church, and there flashed into Timothy's mind a thought of those barbarian hordes who were on the loose throughout the Western world, pillaging, burning, ravaging, and now about to threaten his own city. Could he love them? He would try. St. Stephen would teach him to pray for them.

His thoughts were wandering, until suddenly he saw that the subdeacon who was to read the Epistle had already mounted the pulpit on the south side of the chancel, and was announcing the lesson from the Book of Acts. Timothy listened with rapt intentness to the familiar story of the vision of the first martyr at his stoning. The vision was the theme of the soloist's jubilant chant sung from the step of the pulpit when the lesson was finished—the *Gradual* chant (from *gradus*, meaning a "step"):

> Alleluia! Alleluia!
> I see the heavens opened,
> And Jesus standing at the right hand of God.
> Alleluia! Alleluia!
> Thou hast placed, O Lord, upon his head
> A crown of precious stone.
> Alleluia! Alleluia!

Timothy wished that these triumphal cadences would never end. But already a new procession was forming. One of the deacons, having received the bishop's blessing, took the Gospel book from the altar and descended the steps from the apse into the choir. Before him went two taperers and two subdeacons bearing incense to escort him to the pulpit. How gloriously he chanted the holy Gospel from St. Matthew:

> O Jerusalem, Jerusalem, thou that killest the prophets, and stonest them which are sent unto thee, how often would I have gathered thy children together . . . and ye would not! Behold, your house is left unto you desolate. For I say unto you, Ye shall not see me henceforth, till ye shall say, Blessed is he that cometh in the name of the Lord.

Bishop Gregory remained seated on his throne in the apse to deliver his sermon. "Yesterday," he said, "we celebrated the birthday of our Lord and Saviour, His coming amongst us here on earth. Today we celebrate the birthday of His first Martyr, his coming unto his Lord in heaven." He exhorted the flock to emulate the constancy of faith of this valiant witness, to take courage from his example in the face of many threatening dangers. How often, he reminded them, did they supplicate Almighty God in the Church's prayers to defend and preserve His people from all adversities whether of the body or the soul. They must trust, as did St. Stephen, in the heavenly armor of prayer against all earthly foes. Surely God would supply them plentifully and reward them bountifully if they but remained faithful and steadfast. In particular He shielded them with the grace of these holy mysteries now about to be offered and consecrated with the word of Christ:

> This is my Body, says the Lord. But you also are called His Body. This is your great mystery, which you must keep inviolate and undefiled. For you receive the Body of Christ and you are the Body of Christ. Be therefore what you receive and receive what you are. As the apostle says, "A body hast thou prepared for me. In burnt offerings for sin thou hast had no pleasure. Then said I, Lo, I come to do thy will, O God." Come then to the mystery. "Taste and see how gracious the Lord is; blessed is the man that trusteth in Him." Let unity and fervent charity reign amongst you, that you may be worthy of this great mystery and fellow heirs with all the saints in His eternal Kingdom.

While Timothy pondered these words, taking courage in their comfort, preparations were under way for the mysteries. At the announcement of one of the deacons that all catechumens, all penitents should depart, curtains were drawn across the doors of the basilica, and the draperies in the arches between the nave and aisles were let down. Two deacons spread a linen cloth over the holy Table, covering all four sides, while a subdeacon fetched the chalice to set upon it. The bishop then rose from his seat, saluted the people, and bid the Prayer over the Corporal (i.e., the linen cloth):

> Grant, we beseech thee, Almighty God, that as thy glorious Deacon, Saint Stephen, distinguished himself before all others by following the passion of our Lord Jesus Christ, so may he be a ready helper of our weakness, through the same Jesus Christ our Lord. *Amen.*

The Offertory now began. The lay officials went up to the steps of the apse, followed by all the people—the men to the right, the women to the left—to bring up their oblations of bread and wine, their little buns and flasks. Timothy was thankful that in the rush and excitement of joining the procession he had not forgotten his. The bishop with the presbyters and deacons came down to the foot of the steps to receive the oblations—the bread in linen napkins and the wine in large glass bowls. Meanwhile the choir chanted a psalm. When all the offerings had been gathered, the bishop and presbyters returned to their seats; the deacons laid the oblations of bread on the holy Table and prepared the chalice from the wine that was offered, adding to it a cruet of water which was the special offering of the choir.

The bishop washed his hands, saying as he did so the verse of the psalmist:

> I will wash my hands in innocency, O Lord;
> and so will I go to thine altar;
> That I may show the voice of thanksgiving,
> and tell of all thy wondrous works.

Now coming forward from his throne to the holy Table he stretched forth his hands and bade the people pray that his sacrifice and theirs might be acceptable to God the Father, to the praise of His Name and the benefit of His Church. Then in a low, quiet voice, inaudible except to those standing immediately near him, he said the *Secret*, a prayer commending to God the oblations of His people. Curtains were now drawn around three sides of the Table, between the pillars of the baldachin which protected it, thus shutting off from the people any view of the bishop's act of consecration. The awesome mystery of Christ's coming to be the food of the faithful began to be enacted.

Timothy sang heartily with the choir and people the familiar responses to the bishop's call to "Lift up your hearts." When they reached the thrice-holy, the *Sanctus*, everyone felt the thrill of pure and perfect adoration, as though the veil between heaven and earth had truly lifted and all were joined with the choirs of angels and archangels, of holy patriarchs, prophets, and martyrs in eternal hymning of the glory and majesty of the eternal Trinity. Suddenly, all was silent. Only the faint murmur of the bishop and his presbyters could be heard as they said together the mystic words behind the veiled altar:

> . . . This oblation of our service and of thy whole family, we beseech thee, O Lord, graciously to receive . . . that we be numbered in the flock of thine elect. Which oblation, we beseech thee, O God, in all things to make blessed

. . . that it may become to us the Body and Blood of thy most beloved Son.

We thy servants do offer unto thy most excellent Majesty, of thine own gifts, a pure offering, a holy offering, an undefiled offering, the holy bread of eternal life, and the cup of everlasting salvation. . . . Accept them as thou didst hold accepted the gifts of thy righteous servant Abel, and the sacrifice of our forefather Abraham, and that which thy high priest Melchizedek offered unto thee.

Remember also, O Lord, thy servants and handmaidens who are gone before us with the sign of faith, and rest in the sleep of peace. . . . Grant them a place of refreshment, of light, and of peace. And unto us sinners also . . . vouchsafe to grant some part and fellowship with thy holy Apostles and Martyrs. . . .

Through him, and with him, and in him, be unto thee, O God the Father Almighty, in the unity of the Holy Spirit, all honour and glory, world without end.

At the last phrase the bishop raised his voice that the people might be ready to say their *Amen*, and give to one another the kiss of peace.

A silver paten was brought to the bishop that he might break the loaves and lay the portions upon it for the communion. Slowly he said the Lord's Prayer, to each petition of which the people responded *Amen*. When the bishop and his clergy had finished making their communions, the people went forward again to the steps where they made their offerings, now to receive them back as hallowed mysteries of the Lord's Body and Blood. And the choir sang the communion psalm with its antiphon:

I see the heavens opened,
And Jesus standing at the right hand of God.
Alleluia!

As Timothy went up with his fellow worshippers, he felt a new strength, a fresh resolve, a steadier hope. Standing with bowed head, and hands outstretched to form a cross, he received his piece of holy Bread, and sipped the Wine from one of the large bowls into which some of the consecrated Wine of the chalice had been poured. The warmth of loving grace filled his whole body and spirit, and he heard a voice within him that would not be silenced say: "Leave your law books. Go forth to the heathen barbarian. Lo, I shall be with you." And Timothy said, "Amen. So be it Lord, according to thy will."

Fortunately for Timothy, filled with eagerness to start upon his new vocation, the service was not long in concluding. When all had communicated, the bishop returned to the holy Table and said a brief Collect:

> Grant, O Lord, that the mysteries which we have received may be our defense; and that, by the prayers of thy blessed martyr Saint Stephen, we may be confirmed and strengthened with thine everlasting protection; through our Lord Jesus Christ. *Amen.*

One of the deacons sang, "Go, you are dismissed"; but the people waited until the bishop had returned in procession to the sacristy, for he blessed them as he passed them on the way.

THREE

THE MERITS OF

HIS DEATH AND PASSION

A.D. 1400

It was ten o'clock Whitsun morning. The bells were sounding from the tower of St. Mary's. Mass would soon begin. Richard de Courcy and his lady were riding with their attendants into the churchyard. They were in good time. As they dismounted to enter the church the village folk, who were their tenants, bowed to acknowledge their lord of the manor and his gracious consort. They had been awaiting his arrival, standing about in the churchyard conversing about the latest happenings in the neighborhood. Some of them, to be sure, had come a half-hour early and were already inside, where they had been listening to the priests and clerks sing the Matins office.

Richard and his wife went at once to their seats in the choir where they were accustomed to sit during Mass. The other folk remained in the nave, the more aged and infirm sitting on the few benches that rested against the pillars between nave and aisles, the others standing informally wherever they found it convenient to see the altar. The clergy and their assistant clerks were already in the midst of the choir, blessing the holy water mixed with salt, which they sprinkled about the sanctuary and choir in preparation for the Mass—a symbolic act suggesting the purity of heart with which all worshippers should approach the holy Sacrament.

Since this Sunday was one of the chief festivals of the year, there was a solemn procession about the church. It formed at the foot of the altar steps, then passed through the choir out into the nave, first going down the south aisle and up the center of the nave, then down the north aisle and up the nave again to the entrance of the chancel. At the head of the procession was one of the clerks carrying a cross. Behind him another clerk was swinging a thurible with incense. Then followed in order the three ministers of the Mass in red silk copes, and four choir boys singing the hymn *Salve festa dies:*

> Hail thee, festival day! blest day that art
> hallowed for ever;
> Day whereon God from heav'n shone in
> the world with his grace.

Before re-entering the chancel the procession stopped to make a "station" before the rood or crucifix that surmounted the carved wooden screen, which separated the chancel from the nave. For it was only by the merits of the Cross that men might go their way rejoicing. The vicar chanted an antiphon:

> Holy fire has come not to consume but to illumine,
> and to give gifts of tongues to the apostles,
> that by their mouth all nations may be reborn.
> *Alleluia!*

As the procession went up into the choir to the steps of
the altar, he sang another:

> The day of Pentecost has come. *Alleluia!*
> The Holy Spirit appeared in tongues of fire,
>   and rested upon the disciples,
> And gave them grace to preach
>   and testify in all the world.
> Whosoever repents and is baptized shall be saved.
>   *Alleluia!*

Richard, like his fellow worshippers, was none too
versed in Latin. But though he did not get the sense of
every word that was being sung, he felt no less the joyous
spirit evoked by this holy day when Christendom was
born. And there was much to incite and feed his devotion apart from the spoken word. The pictures both on
walls and in windows that met his eye, as he followed
the procession about the church, were as instructive as
they were colorful—scenes illustrating Bible stories, the
lives of the saints, the sacraments, the seven virtues and
the seven deadly vices.[1] Most impressive of all the frescoes, though Richard could not see it from his seat in the
choir, was the Last Judgment depicted over the chancel
arch (above the rood), with its realistic expressions of
joy and doom on the faces of the blessed and the
damned, as the case may be, a solemn warning of that

> Day of wrath, Day of mourning,
> When fulfilled the prophets' warning,
> Heaven and earth in ashes burning!

---

[1] The four cardinal virtues: temperance, fortitude, justice, and prudence;
and the three theological virtues: faith, hope, and charity. The seven
deadly sins: pride, envy, anger, sloth, avarice, gluttony, and lust.

While the vicar and his assistants were changing from their copes to the Mass vestments and saying before the altar their preparatory devotions for the Mass—the *Veni, Creator Spiritus*, "Come, Holy Ghost, our souls inspire"—Richard turned his glance about the chancel as he repeated to himself his own private preparation, the "Our Father" and the "Hail Mary." The eastern half of the chancel, raised one step above the level of the choir, was the sanctuary proper. It symbolized the Church Triumphant. The choir, of course, represented the Church Expectant, and the nave the Church Militant. The altar symbolized Christ in the midst of His saints. Today it was resplendent with its deep red curtains hung on three sides and the richly embroidered hanging that served as frontal. Lighted candles, suggestive of the "cloven tongues like as of fire," which sat upon the apostles at that first Pentecost, were in abundance. But only two candles stood upon the altar, on either side of a small golden crucifix, to symbolize the two natures, human and divine, of the Lord Himself. Behind the altar a sparkling stained glass window afire with the morning sun portrayed in its three lancet arches the feasts of the Incarnation—the Annunciation, the Nativity, and the Purification. North of the altar and window, a bracket against the east wall held a polychrome statue of the Blessed Virgin, the heavenly patroness of St. Mary's. In the south wall of the sanctuary were set the three *sedilia* or seats for the ministers, and the *piscina* or basin where the celebrant washed his hands before offering the holy sacrifice and where he cleansed the sacred vessels after using them.

The vicar was now mounting the three broad steps

leading up to the altar. Bending over to kiss it, he said the Collect in a low voice:

> Take away from us, we beseech thee, O Lord, all our iniquities, that we may be found worthy to enter into the holy of holies with pure minds, through Jesus Christ our Lord. *Amen.*

As he did so, one of the clerks led the choir boys in the singing of the Introit: "The Spirit of the Lord filleth the world, *Alleluia.*" The other clerk brought to the vicar the thurible that he might cense the altar. Meanwhile Richard opened his *Lay Folks Mass Book*, which he always brought with him to church, that he might follow the service through the brightly colored illuminations of each part of the Mass, and make the vernacular devotions in his English mother tongue which the book suggested. Very few of the parishioners owned such a guide book and help to the service. But then, many of them could not even read English, and if they could, they would have had no means to procure such a book; for the copying of books by hand made them very scarce and expensive.

When the clerks and choir boys had finished the Introit and started singing the *Kyrie eleison*, Richard opened to the proper page and read to himself the confession:

> I know to God full of might,
> And to his mother, maiden bright,
> And to all his hallowed dear,
> In many sins of divers manner,
> And to thee, Father ghostly,
> That I have sinned largely,
> In thought, in speech, and in delight,
> In word, in work, I am to wit,

And worthy for to blame,
For falsely I have tak'n God's name.
Therefore I pray Saint Mary
And all thy hallowed specially,
And the priests, to pray for me,
That God have mercy and pity,
Of my misdeeds that much is,
For his manhood and godness,
Of me that wretched, sinful is,
To give me grace of forgiveness.

The vicar now intoned the *Gloria in excelsis*, and Richard.
turning the page of his book, followed the singing in his
English verses:

Joy be unto God in heaven,
With all kinds mirth that men may name,
And peace in earth all men to tell,
That righteous are, and of good will.

And Richard took a furtive glance at that Nativity scene
in the eastern window as if to hear the angels joining
their chorus with the choir.

After the vicar had said the Collect for the day, beseeching God by His Holy Spirit to give us " a right judgment in all things" that so we may evermore "rejoice in
his holy comfort" and strength, the subdeacon read the
Epistle from the front of the altar, standing as was his
wont on the lowest step. Richard knew he was telling of
that first coming of the Spirit to give the apostles power
to preach to all men in their own tongues "the wonderful
works of God." He silently thanked God that his own
English nation had long since received this blessed word
of forgiveness and grace. As he meditated on the riches

of Christ's merits to heal all his sins and reward him with
eternal bliss, the choir sang the *Gradual* psalm and the
Golden Sequence, the great Whitsun hymn invoking the

PLATE V

The Celebration of the Mass
Psalter of King Alfonso V of Aragon
(Courtesy of the Trustees of the British Museum)

manifold gifts of the Holy Spirit, "Come, thou Holy
Spirit, come!":

> Heal our wounds, our strength renew;
> On our dryness pour thy dew;
>   Wash the stains of guilt away:
> Bend the stubborn heart and will;
> Melt the frozen, warm the chill;
>   Guide the steps that go astray.

· 41 ·

During the Sequence hymn the subdeacon repaired to the little chapel on the north side of the chancel to prepare the bread and wine.

The Gospel procession formed immediately at the end of the hymn. The two clerks, one with a taper, the other bearing incense, and the subdeacon escorted the deacon from the altar, where he had gone to pick up the Book, through the choir out to the pulpit at the southeast corner of the nave. At the deacon's announcement of the Gospel lesson from St. John the choir sang the "Glory be to thee, O Lord." Facing toward the north—the traditional land of the heathen—the deacon solemnly chanted the sacred lesson. Richard and his fellow worshippers stood erect and attentive during the Gospel (only for the Gospel and the Creed were they all required to stand), but he let his eye fall upon his book for a moment that he might say one of the brief prayers suggested at this place:

> Jesus, my lord, grant me grace,
> Of amendment might and space,
> Thy word to keep, and all thy will,
> The good to choose, and leave the ill,
> And that it so may be,
> Good Jesus, grant it me. *Amen.*

There was no sermon from the vicar this morning because of the extra length of this festal service. Often, however, on ordinary Sundays he would give them brief instruction on the Creed or the Lord's Prayer, or tell them a story of one of the saints. But the vicar did come to the pulpit and lead his flock in the Bidding of the Bedes, the English Bidding Prayer for the King and his councilors, for the clergy and all estates in Christ's Church,

PLATE VI

The Canon of the Mass, The Tiptoft Missal

(Courtesy of The Pierpont Morgan Library, New York)

both living and dead, for the sick and afflicted and the dying, for fair weather and a good harvest. After each group of biddings, everyone said the Lord's Prayer.

Returning to the altar, with the deacon and sub-deacon on either side, the vicar intoned the Nicene Creed:

Credo in unum Deum. I believe in one God.

The choir took up the rest. Richard and the other wor-shippers occupied themselves by saying quietly the Apostles' Creed, which they knew by heart in English. All made a profound bow during the phrases: "And was incarnate by the Holy Ghost of the Virgin Mary . . . And was crucified . . . He suffered and was buried"— that by this gesture they might express the deep humilia-tion of God's Son in coming into the world to suffer for our sins.

The Offertory followed. The subdeacon went to the chapel, to get the paten and chalice he had prepared, and brought them to the deacon, who in turn handed them to the priest to place and offer on the altar. While the choir sang the Offertory psalm the people came up one by one to give the vicar at the altar steps their "mass-penny." It was both an oblation and an alms, for the priest used the money to supply what was needed for the altar service and to relieve the poor and needy of the parish. Richard made his offering with the others. When he returned to his seat he picked up his book again to continue his devotions, while the priest censed the obla-tions and washed his hands, and said the secret prayers commending the sacrifice of the Church to Almighty God. In his book Richard read:

Have meditation how our Lord the Saviour of all man-kind most willingly offered himself to his eternal Father to be sacrifice and oblation for man's Redemption, and offer yourself to him again both body and soul which he so dearly bought. Render all the thanks of your heart that it would please his goodness to be ransom for your trespass and sins.

The celebrant was now singing the *Sursum corda,* bidding them to lift up their hearts and join with angelic choirs in praise. When the last sound of the *Sanctus* and *Hosanna in excelsis* had echoed through the church, everyone knelt down while the priest said secretly the mystic Canon, or consecration of the oblations. Richard followed the directions in his book to render thanks to God for all His good gifts, and especially for his redemption by His Son, to ask pardon for all his sins, and to pray for all Christian people and for his kinsmen, friends, tenants, and servants, for all in sorrow and need.

A bell sounded. The priest had come to the most sacred words of all, the words with which the Lord instituted the holy Sacrament. It was the supreme moment in the service. All looked up eagerly to see the priest lift the host, and then the chalice, when he had said the words:

THIS IS MY BODY

. . .

THIS IS MY BLOOD

Now the oblations were no longer bread and wine but the very Body and Blood of the Redeemer. In adoration of the elevated Host and Cup each offered the best prayers he knew—the "Our Father" and the "Hail Mary." Richard also knew another prayer by heart, which he said at this time:

Loved be thou, king;
And blessed be thou, king;
Of all thy gifts good,
And thanked be thou, king;
Jesus, all my joying,
That for me spilt thy blood,
And died upon the rood,
Thou give me grace to sing
The song of thy loving.

Then, as the priest went on silently to finish the consecration prayer, Richard made his prayers for all the
faithful departed, that they might have a part also in
the Mass to their good and profit. He remembered particularly his parents and forebears, who, like him, had
loved this church and the Mass that was offered in it for
the remedy of their souls and the good of all mankind.

At the conclusion of the Canon of consecration the
priest sang the Lord's Prayer through "lead us not into
temptation." The people responded, "But deliver us from
evil." It was the one Latin phrase they knew well. Then
he gave them the Peace. He kissed the little paddle-
shaped ivory "pax-brede," with its carved image of the
crucifixion, and passed it on to the deacon to kiss. Then
it passed in order to all the people to kiss, that by this
act they might learn that peace and love which should
dwell among them as Christian brethren. While the
people were kissing the "pax-brede," the priest broke the
Host over the chalice, as Christ broke the holy Bread at
the Last Supper. Then he made his communion during
the singing of the *Agnus Dei* by the choir:

O Lamb of God, that takest away the sins of the world,
Have mercy upon us.

O Lamb of God, that takest away the sins of the world,
Grant us thy peace.

No one but the celebrant received communion, for
the people only made their communion once a year, at
Easter, after they had been shriven. The priest therefore
cleansed the vessels at once, while the choir sang the
Communion psalm. When he had washed his hands, he
bade the people to prayer, and said a brief Postcom-
munion Collect:

May the outpouring of the Holy Spirit cleanse our hearts,
O Lord, and render them fruitful by the inward dew of
his grace; through Jesus Christ our Lord. *Amen.*

The deacon sang the ancient dismissal and the priest,
holding the paten in his right hand, blessed the people
as he made the sign of the cross over them. The clergy
retired to the vestry room, while the priest recited to himself, "In the beginning was the Word. . . ." When they
had taken off their vestments they said the *Benedicite:*

O all ye works of the Lord, bless ye the Lord;
Praise him and magnify him for ever. . . .

Richard lingered a bit longer, as though he needed
time to absorb all the richness of this service—its beauty
and grace. He was thinking how he might add to the
adornment of God's house and leave behind his own
memorial in good and pious works. Perhaps another
chapel could be built, on the south side of the chancel
to match the one on the north side. Suddenly, almost
unwillingly, he remembered the many poor folk in the
parish. Yes, before he built a chapel he must provide for
their necessities. For Christ's tender mercies' sake, he
would give and give again.

FOUR

PARTAKERS OF
THIS HOLY COMMUNION

A.D. 1665

Not long after King Charles II's restoration to the throne, James Harrington sailed for the new world on business for the proprietors. He had no idea of settling in the colonies, but quite unexpectedly he found himself in two years' time a pioneer plantation owner. When he returned to England to get his wife and young children, he paid a farewell visit to his parents and relatives at the homestead in Staffordshire. It was late March, a fortnight before he was due to sail again for America. Since Easter came early this year, he was able to share with his kinfolk and friends a last communion in the old parish church where he had been baptized and confirmed. It would be a fitting Godspeed to him and his family for their new venture of life across the sea.

For generations James's forebears had been patrons of St. Luke's parish. The old gray Gothic church had received its present form in the thirteenth century, though some of the foundation stones dated back to Anglo-Saxon times. Most of the medieval furnishings and ornaments, however, had been destroyed during the upheavals of Reformation days. Their last relic, the carved chancel screen, had been demolished only a few years ago in the heyday of Puritanism, the Commonwealth of Oliver Cromwell, when the family temporarily lost their patronage of the church. At the same time the organ had been removed. Neither screen nor organ had as yet been restored in the five years since King Charles's return. But the chancel was now enclosed by a wooden rail of tasteful workmanship. Otherwise the furnishings remained much the same as James had always known them. Their elegance and quality relieved the sober gravity of the old building, shorn of all its medieval color and symbolism.

In the middle of the chancel stood the massive walnut holy Table placed there in Elizabethan days. Usually vested on all sides with a green damask carpet edged with gold silk fringe, the Table was today covered by the fair linen cloth for the Communion. On it was placed the handsome silver service—flagon, paten, chalice, and alms basin—donated by James's great-grandfather. A purple cushion, at the north end of the Table, supported a folio copy of the new 1662 Prayer Book, sumptuously bound in Turkey red leather and closed with a silver clasp. Affixed to the east wall behind the Table was a tablet, required by the Canon Law of the Church, inscribed with the Ten Commandments, the Apostles' Creed, and the Lord's Prayer. Neatly inscribed at the top of the tablet were the royal arms of James I.

The nave was lined on either side by the square-box pews, variously furnished with cushions and hassocks according to the tastes of the several families that occupied them. The Harrington pew, somewhat larger than the others, was located in front on the north side, directly behind the rector's reading desk and stall. A circular staircase connected this stall with the pulpit, which surmounted the reading desk in a two-decker arrangement. Opposite the rector's stall, on the south side, was the reading desk of the parish clerk. St. Luke's clerk, a Mr. John Tewkes, had served for forty years, leading the congregation in its responses and psalm-singing, and assisting the minister in the services. His tenure had lasted without interruption, even during the days of the Puritan Commonwealth.

The Harringtons arrived shortly before ten, the hour of divine service. James's thoughts, as he settled in his familiar place, were full of memories and anticipations. Picking up one of the new Prayer Books—it had been revised since he had last attended here—he leafed through its pages to note any striking changes from the old version. He did not notice the rector when, vested in his surplice, he entered the stall directly in front of him. But the announcement by the clerk of the opening psalm brought him to attention. It was "Old 84th." Reading it out line by line Mr. Tewkes led the people in singing it to the familiar tune "York." Without the support of an organ the choral efforts of the congregation were slightly ragged. But they sang it heartily:

> How pleasant is thy dwelling place,
> O Lord of hosts to me!
> The tabernacles of thy grace,
> how pleasant, Lord, they be!
>
> My soul doth long full sore to go
> into thy courts abroad:

My heart and flesh cry out also
for thee the living God.

For God the Lord, light and defense,
will grace and worship give:
And no good thing will he withhold
from them that purely live.

James wondered, as he sang, how long it would be before he could join such an act of praise and prayer in his new-world home. As yet there was no parish church in the neighborhood of his American plantation.

After the psalm the rector read the opening sentences of Morning Prayer and called the people to confession of their sins. In the Absolution, which followed, he summoned them to prayer that the "rest of our life hereafter may be pure and holy, so that at the last we may come to his eternal joy." In place of the *Venite* the Easter anthems were said: "Christ our Passover is sacrificed for us: therefore let us keep the feast." Then the proper Psalms for Easter Day were recited responsively by the minister and people. They were Psalms 2, 57, and 111. Many verses brought to mind not only the resurrection of the Lord, but also the resurrection of the Church and its magnificent liturgy, after the long years of proscription by the Puritans. So it seemed, at least, to James, who, like all his family, was a staunch adherent of the Church of England. The people had indeed "imagined a vain thing," and their rulers had "taken counsel together, against the Lord and against his Anointed." But God had been merciful. Under the shadow of His wings, His people had taken refuge "until this tyranny be overpast."

The works of the Lord are great:
    sought out of all them that have pleasure therein.
His work is worthy to be praised, and had in honour:
    and his righteousness endureth for ever.
The merciful and gracious Lord hath so done his
    marvellous works: that they ought to be had
    in remembrance.

The first lesson from the Old Testament, customarily read by the clerk, was taken from the twelfth chapter of Exodus, the account of the institution of the Passover. At its conclusion the congregation stood and joined in saying the *Te Deum*. Then the rector read the second lesson from the New Testament, Romans 6, concerning our baptism with Christ into death that we might rise with Him in newness of life. The phrase "newness of life" struck James with unwonted freshness, for that in truth was what he would seek in the new world. The *Benedictus* was recited after the lesson, and the rector concluded the Morning Prayer with the Creed and prayers.

The Litany was now begun. James could hardly believe that it was almost twenty years since he had heard this majestic supplication. A few words and phrases in it were new to him. "Rebellion" and "schism" were now added to the deprecations against sedition and heresy. Instead of "Bishops, Pastors, and Ministers," the Litany spoke of "Bishops, Priests, and Deacons." No doubt, the revisers of the liturgy had the late Puritan regime in mind when they made these changes. It was good, too, to hear once more the suffrage for "thy servant Charles, our most gracious King and governor."

Immediately after the conclusion of the Litany, the rector went to the sanctuary, to the north end of the

PLATE VII

Divine Service, St. Margaret's, Westminster

holy Table, to begin the Communion service. Meanwhile the clerk and congregation engaged themselves in singing the second part of "Old 33rd" to the tune "Windsor":

> Blessed are they to whom the Lord
> as God and guide is known:
> Whom he doth chuse of meet accord,
> to take them as his own.
>
> Wherefore our soul doth whole depend
> on God our strength and stay:
> He is our shield us to defend,
> and drive all darts away.

The Lord's Prayer and the Collect for Purity were followed by the recital of the Ten Commandments. To each Commandment the people joined the clerk in making response: "Lord, have mercy upon us, and incline our hearts to keep this law." Then the rector read the Collect for the King and the Collect for the day:

> Almighty God, who through thine only-begotten Son Jesus Christ hast overcome death, and opened unto us the gate of everlasting life; we humbly beseech thee, that, as by thy special grace preventing us thou dost put into our minds good desires, so by thy continual help we may bring the same to good effect; through Jesus Christ our Lord, who liveth and reigneth with thee and the Holy Ghost, ever one God, world without end. *Amen.*

The Collects ended, the clerk stood up in his stall to read the Epistle from St. Paul's letter to the Colossians. The rector then read the Gospel account in St. John of the visit of the disciples to the empty tomb. After all had joined in the Nicene Creed, and announcements had been made of the Easter week services, the rector repaired to the sacristy to exchange his surplice for the black preaching gown.

The congregation listened with close attention to the sermon. One part of it was particularly noteworthy— where the rector explained the relation of our Easter faith to the Sacrament of the Lord's Body and Blood:

> By the means of this Sacrament our Bodies are made capable of the resurrection to Life and eternal Glory. For when we are *externally* and symbolically in the Sacrament, and by Faith and the Spirit of God *internally* united to Christ, and made partakers of His Body and Blood, we are joined and made one with Him, who did rise again; and when the Head is risen, the Members shall not see corruption for ever, but rise again after the pattern of our Lord. If by the Sacrament we are really united and made one with Christ, then it shall be to us in our proportion as it was to Him; we shall rise again, and we shall enter into Glory.
>
> . . . By this Holy Ministry we are joined and partake of Christ's Body and Blood, and then we become spiritually one Body, and therefore shall receive in our Bodies all the effects of that spiritual Union; the chief of which in relation to our Bodies, is Resurrection from the Grave.

Seldom had the people of St. Luke's been so moved by the rector's penetrating insight into the deepest mysteries of our faith. For James Harrington it was a spiritual resurrection to "newness of life," sealed with a firm resolve that in his new home he would bend every effort to assure himself, his family, and his neighbors the ministration of these mysteries of Word and Sacrament. In his stirred imagination, a new parish in a new world was born.

PLATE VIII

Holy Communion

(From Nathaniel Crouch, *Divine Banquet*, London, 1696)

After his sermon the rector vested again in his surplice and returned to the holy Table to announce the Offertory: "Let your light so shine before men, that they may see your good works, and glorify your Father which is in heaven." The clerk then took up the reading of the other Offertory Sentences, while the wardens gathered the alms of the people. James was privileged to serve this morning in place of his father in receiving the people's charitable gifts and presenting them to the rector. Meanwhile, the rector prepared the paten and chalice with the bread and wine. When he had received the alms, he bade the people to prayer for "the whole state of Christ's Church militant here in earth"—for its unity and concord, for the King, for bishops and curates, for the congregation present, and for all in need, ending with a recalling of the faithful departed and a prayer that the congregation have grace "to follow their good examples."

A lengthy Exhortation to those "that mind to come to the Holy Communion" was addressed to the people, reminding them of their need for "a true penitent heart and lively faith" before presuming to eat of the bread and drink of the cup. Then with an Invitation to make "humble confession to Almighty God, meekly kneeling," the rector led the congregation in a general Confession. The Absolution was pronounced and the "comfortable words" of Scripture were read, assuring them of God's love and pardon for Christ's sake.

Now followed the ancient bidding:

> Lift up your hearts.
> Let us give thanks . . .

and the people's responses. The Easter Day preface—"but chiefly are we bound to praise thee for the glorious Resurrection of thy Son"—led up to the *Sanctus*. The rector then knelt to say the Prayer, "We do not presume to come to this thy Table, O merciful Lord, trusting in our own righteousness." Now the linen cloth covering the paten and chalice was removed, and the Prayer of Consecration began. It was an impressive memorial of the Lord's one sacrifice made upon the Cross for the "sins of the whole world," to be perpetually remembered "until his coming again." With a petition that those who received "these creatures of bread and wine," in remembrance of Him, might be "partakers of his most blessed Body and Blood," the Prayer moved on to a recital of the Lord's institution. The rector, as he said these words, broke the bread and held the cup in the sight of all the people. They responded with a fervent *Amen*.

The rector knelt at the Table to make his own communion, and afterward all the people came to the rail to receive in their hands the consecrated Bread and to drink the sacred Wine. To each communicant he said words calling them to remembrance and thanksgiving.

> Take and eat this in rememberance . . . and feed
> on him in thy heart by faith with thanksgiving.
> Drink this in remembrance . . . and be thankful.

At this high point of communion James's thought could not suppress the keen anticipation of the coming years. He could see clearly in his imagination the same experience of grateful remembrance in the lives of neighbors, friends, and kinsmen yet to be. He prayed, momentarily, yet no less earnestly, that such blessings would continue to be his across the sea.

After the communion, the sacred elements that remained were covered once more with the fair linen cloth, and the rector led the people in the Lord's Prayer. Another prayer followed, a prayer of oblation, beseeching God to accept this "sacrifice of praise and thanksgiving," and offering up to Him the souls and bodies of all His people in "a reasonable, holy, and lively sacrifice." The hymn, "Glory be to God on high," was then said by the whole congregation, standing, as a closing doxology of praise. Then the people knelt once more to receive the Blessing of peace, to keep their hearts and minds "in the knowledge and love of God." While the rector consumed the remaining consecrated elements, the clerk led the people in a final psalm, "Old 100th":

> All people that on earth do dwell,
> > Sing to the Lord with cheerful voice:
> Him serve with fear, his praise forth tell,
> > Come ye before him and rejoice.
>
> For why? the Lord our God is good,
> > His mercy is for ever sure;
> His truth at all times firmly stood,
> > And shall from age to age endure.

In London, ten days later, just before he was about to sail, James received a messenger with a package from J. Coatsworthe, silversmith. Attached to it was a note addressed to him, in his father's handwriting:

> My dear Son: Herewith you will be pleased to accept a silver Communion service, the gift of your friends in St. Luke's. We trust that God's providence will preserve you safely in the plantations, and raise up for Him in a distant land the praises worthy of His holy Name. To which I add the affectionate Godspeed of your loving father,
> > Henry Harrington, Esq.

FIVE

DO THIS
IN REMEMBRANCE

A.D. 1830

St. John's Church was located on the northeast corner of Elm and Washington Streets, two blocks west of the main business intersection of the town. The first Episcopal services had been held in the community in 1734 by a missionary of the Society for the Propagation of the Gospel, in the home of a prosperous merchant. In due time a small frame church was built. During the American Revolution the British chaplain held services in it for his troops, but none of the townspeople attended. Shortly after the evacuation of the British, the edifice was burned. The sole relic of this period, highly prized by the parish, was a Prayer Book with the prayer for the King scratched out and one for the Continental Congress substituted in its place.

After the Revolution the parish suffered evil days for lack of a minister, but in 1823 a traveling missionary of the Domestic and Foreign Missionary Society settled in the community and reorganized the parish. Within two years' time a brick church had been erected, and a year later the building was ready for consecration by the bishop. It was a plain, straightforward meeting house in the neoclassical style of "colonial" times, with no trace of the Gothic features which were beginning to be popular in church edifices. The interior was equally simple, with its two rows of white, box-shaped pews, each fitted and furnished according to the taste of the family renting it. The large, arched windows with their plain glass let in sufficient light.

At the east end of the church, dominating the whole interior, was a high pulpit, made of mahogany, over which hung an octagonal sounding board. It was approached by a steep flight of steps that connected it with the vestry room in the rear. In front of the pulpit at a lower level was a wide reading desk, commodious enough for at least three persons. On it rested a large Bible and Prayer Book. Immediately in front of the reading desk on the floor level was a Communion Table, on three sides of which ran a communion rail to form a small but comfortable chancel. This arrangement of pulpit, reading desk, and holy Table was a fairly recent fashion in church interior designing, intended to enhance the significance of the Holy Communion. Heretofore, it had been customary to place the Table either behind the pulpit or at the other end of the edifice. To the right of the chancel was located the baptismal font. The grouping together of these furnishings was thus symbolical of the primary elements in the Church's worship—the preaching of the Word and the administration of the Sacraments. If the pulpit seemed disproportionate in size, that also was symbolical. Every Sunday there was a sermon, but the

Holy Communion was observed only four times a year.

Of other ornaments in the church, there were none—no crosses, no candles, no flowers. True, there were affixed to the wall on either side of the pulpit two plaques, one with the Ten Commandments, the other with the Apostles' Creed and Lord's Prayer inscribed on them—those chief things "which a Christian ought to know and believe to his soul's health." The parish also boasted a fine new organ, the largest in the town. It was located in the gallery over the entrance at the west end where the small volunteer choir sat to lead the congregational singing of hymns. There was no chanting and no anthem at the Sunday services. The choir, of course, was not vested. Had the idea of doing so occurred to anyone it would have been considered "popish."

On Sunday, October 3rd, being that year the Seventeenth Sunday after Trinity, the congregation gathered as was their custom for divine service at the hour of 10:30 A.M. Usually the service consisted of Morning Prayer, Litany, Ante-Communion, with a sermon; but today the quarterly Communion service was in order (the other three occasions of its celebration during the year being Christmas, Easter, and Whitsunday). Preparations for the Communion were being made by the sexton when the congregation began to arrive. He covered the holy Table with a fair linen cloth and placed upon it the paten and chalice already prepared with the elements, leavened bread and wine unmixed with water. Another linen cloth was used to cover them until such time as they should be needed in the service. Everything was in readiness.

The rector arrived in good time and, after greeting

some of the parishioners already in their pews, retired to the vestry room to don his ample white surplice. When the peal of the bell in the steeple had ended, he mounted to the reading desk and announced the opening hymn— a metrical version of Psalm 105:

> O render thanks, and bless the Lord,
>   Invoke his sacred Name;
> Acquaint the nations with his deed,
>   His matchless deeds proclaim.
>
> Rejoice in his Almighty Name,
>   Alone to be adored;
> And let their hearts o'erflow with joy
>   That humbly seek the Lord.

Facing the people from the reading desk, but standing or kneeling as the rubrics directed, the rector read Morning Prayer and the Litany. He began with the opening sentence: "When the wicked man turneth away from his wickedness that he hath committed, and doeth that which is lawful and right, he shall save his soul alive." Then he exhorted his people to acknowledge and confess their sins "with an humble, lowly, penitent, and obedient heart." Thus the congregation prepared themselves with fitting confession to render thanks and praise, to hear God's most holy Word, and to ask those things "requisite and necessary, as well for the body as the soul." The *Venite* and psalms were said responsively; the canticles read after the two lessons were *Te Deum* and *Jubilate*. The appointed lessons were I Samuel 12 and Luke 13.

The Collect for the day was omitted from its usual place in Morning Prayer as it was to come later in the Communion service. Immediately after the Prayer for the President, the rector passed to the Litany. When the Litany was finished, the congregation sang another hymn, the first section of Psalm 119:

> How blest are they who always keep
> The pure and perfect way;
> Who never from the sacred paths
> Of God's commandments stray!

During the last stanza of the psalm the rector descended from the reading desk to the chancel and took his place at the north side of the holy Table. From this position he read the Ante-Communion.

After the Collect for Purity the rector rehearsed with the people the Ten Commandments:

> God spake these words, and said, I am the Lord thy God:
> Thou shalt have none other gods but me.

To each commandment the people responded, "Lord, have mercy upon us, and incline our hearts to keep this law." The Epistle and Gospel both stressed the virtues of humility and compassion in our dealings one with another, and gave concreteness to the petition of the Collect, that God "make us continually to be given to all good works." The Creed was omitted, as it had already been said in Morning Prayer. During the singing of another metrical psalm the rector retired to the vestry room to exchange his surplice for the black gown and muslin bands which he always wore when preaching.

In his sermon that morning the rector tried to relate the dominant themes of the service to the meaning of the Holy Communion. Among other things he said:

> The Lord's Supper is not instituted for the nourishment of the body, but for the refreshment of the soul; the soul therefore must be put in a proper disposition to receive

PLATE IX

Interior, Trinity Church
Newport, Rhode Island

(Henry A. Curtis)

· 65 ·

it, and feed upon it. It is a lively representation of the
death of Christ for the sins of mankind; and therefore
the soul must possess a just sense of the sufferings of
Christ and his love to mankind, and also an humble and
lively faith, and hope in his merits. It is an office of praise
and thanksgiving for the greatest blessings; redemption
from eternal death; restoration to the favour of God, and
a title to everlasting life; to celebrate it aright, therefore,
the soul must come prepared with a due sense, both of the
extreme misery of our condition, without a redeemer, and
also of the blessings and benefits to which we are entitled
through Christ. It is also a memorial of our deliverance
from the power of sin, and is the means by which we
become partakers of the spirit of God: we should therefore bring with us to this ordinance not only a willing-
ness, but a desire for deliverance from the power of our
sins, and for the assistance of God's Holy Spirit to subdue
them, with firm resolutions to improve his grace.

In this holy Sacrament, we behold the supreme claim
which Christ has to our homage and obedience, since he
bought us with the price of his own blood; and therefore
we cannot partake of this ordinance aright, without a just
sense of our obligations to serve and obey him as our Lord
and Master, and without resigning ourselves to his will.
The holy Sacrament, under the most impressive and
affecting emblems, sets before us the covenant of mercy
and pardon, to which God is pleased to admit mankind,
on condition of their repentance and amendment; and
hence arises the indispensable necessity of repenting of
our past sins, and entering into resolutions of obedience
for the future. In this holy supper we hold communion
with our fellow Christians, as brethren, and members of
the same body under Christ our head; and hence it follows, that love, and unity, must be necessary qualifica-
tions for a right participation of this sacred ordinance.

PLATE X

Holy Communion

(From The Book of Common Prayer, New York, 1827)

The sermon ended, the rector repaired to the vestry to remove his gown and bands and put on once more his surplice. Then returning to the chancel, again to the north side of the Table, he began the Offertory with the sentence: "Let your light so shine before men, that they may see your good works, and glorify your Father which is in heaven." While he read out slowly and solemnly several of these Offertory Sentences from the Holy Scriptures, exhorting the people to give of their substance generously and ungrudgingly, the churchwardens received the alms of the people in the great brass alms basins provided for the purpose. Ordinarily a collection was not taken at the Sunday service, unless it were a special offering for missions—since the parish was supported by pew rentals, special donations, and church fairs. But always at the Communion an offering of alms for the poor and needy was received.

When the churchwardens had finished collecting the alms and had deposited them on the floor at the head of the aisle, the rector bade the people to prayer "for the whole (i.e., healthy) state of Christ's Church militant." This was followed by the long Exhortation—which seemed to sum up so perfectly what was said from the pulpit:

> . . . And to the end that we should always remember the exceeding great love of our Master, and only Saviour, Jesus Christ, thus dying for us, and the innumerable benefits which by his precious blood-shedding he hath obtained for us; he hath instituted and ordained holy mysteries, as pledges of his love, and for a continual remembrance of his death, to our great and endless comfort.

The sense of comfort, or strengthening, continued

as the rector read the Invitation to all who "truly and earnestly repent," being in love and charity with their neighbors, and intending to lead a new life. He bade them to "draw near with faith, and take this holy Sacrament to your comfort." He kneeled with them for their common confession of sin, then stood to assure them of God's pardon "to confirm and strengthen" them in all goodness. Comfortable, strengthening words of our Lord and the apostles were read from the Scriptures, assuring them that "Christ Jesus came into the world to save sinners."

Fortified with these pledges, all join in the ancient, traditional hymn of thanksgiving—"Lift up your hearts" —uniting the worshippers of heaven and earth in adoration of the Holy One whose glory fills all created beings and things. A pause is made in these exultant praises while the rector kneels to say in the name of all a Prayer of Humble Access, of their unworthiness for these "manifold and great mercies." Then standing again, still at the north end of the Table, half facing the people, he uncovers the sacred vessels and begins the Prayer of Consecration, taking up the theme of the *Sanctus* in an offering of "all glory" for the wondrous redemption of God's Son upon the Cross, and the perpetual memorial which He left of it to His Church. As he recites the Words of Institution he breaks the bread and lifts the cup before the people as Christ did at the Last Supper and thus celebrates the memorial He commanded us to make "in remembrance of his blessed passion and precious death, his mighty resurrection and glorious ascension, rendering . . . most hearty thanks for the innumerable benefits procured unto us by the same."

The thought of remembrance continued in the Invocation now pronounced over the holy gifts, that the Father would bless and sanctify them with His Word and Holy Spirit, that those receiving them according to the Lord's institution, "in remembrance of his Death and Passion, may be partakers of his most blessed Body and Blood." Finally, the solemn Prayer concluded with a dedication of the worshippers, their souls and bodies, to the service of the Lord, beseeching Him to grant them His mercy, grace, and heavenly benediction. And all responded with a hearty *Amen.* An attentive and earnest devotion had gripped the people throughout this stately form with its phrases both venerable and affecting. As if to give expression to their feelings before coming forward to receive the consecrated Food, all joined in singing the familiar hymn:

> My God, and is thy table spread?
>   And does thy cup with love o'erflow?
> Thither be all thy children led,
>   And let them thy sweet mercies know!
>
> O let thy table honour'd be,
>   And furnish'd well with joyful guests!
> And may each soul salvation see,
>   That here its holy pledges tastes.
>
> Nor let thy spreading gospel rest,
>   Till through the world thy truth has run,
> Till with this bread all men be blest,
>   Who see the light or feel the sun.

The minister made his communion while the congregation came up to the chancel rail to kneel and receive the Bread and the Cup, the Body and Blood of the Lord. To each one separately he said the words of administration—calling them to eat and drink "in remembrance" and "with thanksgiving." When all had returned to their accustomed places, he covered what remained of the sacred elements with a linen cloth. Refreshed and restored to God's favor, all repeated after the rector, phrase by phrase, the "Our Father," the first prayer they took upon their lips after communion. Then the rector said a brief prayer of thanksgiving, summing up the praise and petition of the whole service, and all stood up at its conclusion to say with him the *Gloria in excelsis*. When the final Blessing had been said, the rector beckoned to the churchwardens to come up to the chancel rail and partake with him of the consecrated Bread and Wine that remained after the communion.

The service concluded, as it had begun, with a psalm of praise, the 135th:

> O praise the Lord with one consent,
>   And magnify his Name;
> Let all the servants of the Lord
>   His worthy praise proclaim.
>
> Their just returns of thanks to God
>   Let grateful Israel pay;
> Nor let anointed Aaron's race
>   To bless the Lord delay.
>
> Let all with thanks his wondrous works
>   In Sion's courts proclaim;
> Let them in Salem, where he dwells,
>   Exalt his holy Name.

SIX

THAT HOLY FELLOWSHIP

A.D. 1970

The parish dedicated its new church to St. Paul—not because his name was a favorite one for Episcopal churches. No, it was because St. Paul was a worker, a manual laborer, who was also a busy missionary. Also St. Paul taught us that the Church is the Body of Christ, the fellowship of all sorts and conditions of men, united in faith and love by the Spirit of the living Lord. St. Paul's parish was very much a "body," members one of another in common work and in a common missionary purpose. It was located in the heart of a thriving industrial community, which had known its share, not too long since, of strife and even violence. But one day a few Christian laymen among both employers and employees had met together and agreed that cooperation and negotiation were the better way and that a parish church established in their midst would help to foster a spirit of reconciliation and concord. That is how St. Paul's parish began.

Several plans for the church building had been thoroughly discussed. Everyone agreed that the edifice should be modern in design and construction, in keeping with the simple, sturdy, and spacious homes, schools, and factories of the neighborhood. Also it must conform to the basic pattern of the liturgy as a common action of all the people about a common Table. No obstruction of any kind should stand in the way of any worshipper's being able to see the entire Eucharistic drama. The cruciform plan was therefore rejected, despite its age-long symbolism and associations, in favor of a design more nearly akin to the ancient basilica church. At one end of a spacious, open nave was placed a wide, commodious sanctuary, but a few steps above the level of the nave. Three broad steps within the sanctuary lead up to the altar, a stone Table placed in the center of the sanctuary, adorned only with the fair linen cloth and two stately candles. Directly over the altar was hung from the ceiling an encircled cross portraying the Christ vested as King and Priest.

The seating of the choir was also arranged after the pattern of the ancient basilica. Since their function is first and foremost to lead the congregational singing it seemed appropriate to place them in the body of the church. But the choir also performs a special ministry of its own, hence it was thought fitting that they be seated in front of the people, nearest the sanctuary, on the level of the nave floor but enclosed within a low chancel screen. The great center aisle of the church, however, was open all the way down the nave through the choir chancel to the entrance of the sanctuary. On the "Gospel" side of the choir screen was placed the pulpit, where God's Word was read and preached. It could be mounted from either side of the screen.

Every Sunday morning at 9:30 the whole parish— children, young people, grown-ups—attended the parish

Eucharist. Many came a half-hour early to stay and sing together Morning Prayer within the choir. Sometimes a clergyman conducted it, sometimes one of the laity. The intimacy and informality of the service, made up as it is of psalms, Bible reading, and brief prayers at the beginning of the day, made it particularly popular with those members of the parish who had no opportunity for "Family Prayers." After the Eucharist was over most of the worshippers repaired to the parish house for an informal gathering to welcome visitors and strangers, and to chat about parish activities and accomplishments.

This particular Sunday was "Stir Up" Sunday, the end of the Christian Year, a day of thanksgiving for the blessings of the past year and of eager anticipation for the work of the coming one. There was a special reason for being elated today, since the annual canvass had been subscribed over the top. One of the outstanding features of St. Paul's program was a principle adopted at the very first organization of the parish; namely, every dollar given and spent for the needs of the local church was to be matched by an equal sum contributed to the diocesan and general missionary work of the Church. The idea behind this plan was simply this: if we live in "one world" of interdependent problems and needs, any strength given to the Church's mission afield must of necessity set forward the work at home. No member of Christ's Body can be healthy if other members are sick. The Church's life is an organic whole. Besides, if Christianity means anything, it is that "it is more blessed to give than to receive." Such arguments as these, in any case, had won over a few cautious parishioners who felt that the plan was too idealistic and impractical, particularly for a struggling new parish. The result of the parish's faith and courage had been a consecration on the part of all to sacrificial giving.

Each communicant upon arrival at the church, before going to his seat, stopped at a large table placed near the door, to signify to the vestryman seated there his desire to "make an oblation." The vestryman then placed one of the pieces of bread in the silver breadbox which was to be offered, with the cruets of wine and water and the alms, at the appropriate time in the service, by the chosen representatives of the congregation. Meanwhile the paten and chalice were placed unobtrusively on a small credence table at one side of the sanctuary, until such time as they would be needed. Also on the credence table was a small breadbox containing the breads which the clergy and those who assisted them in the sanctuary and choir were to offer together with the oblations of the people.

Since this Sunday was not a great festival day of the Church Year, there was no procession about the church. The choir came in quietly, two by two, from their vesting room to take their places in the chancel. When all were ready, the congregation stood to join with them in the Introit hymn. Today it was Studdert-Kennedy's stirring song, "Awake, awake to love and work!"—set to a sturdy old American folk-melody. During the singing of the hymn the ministers entered and took their places before the steps leading up to the altar. The rector, who was celebrant, stood in the center; to his right stood the curate, who would serve as gospeller and deacon, to his left a layman to act as epistler and sub-deacon, and on either end a server.

When the last stanza of the hymn, with its thought of "giving, spending, serving," had ended, all knelt while the celebrant said the opening invocation of the Triune God (the Collect for Purity), that by the cleansing and inspiring gift of the Holy Spirit they might all offer to the Father a perfect love and a worthy praise of His holy Name through Jesus Christ our Lord. Then mounting the steps to the center of the altar and turning to the people, he rehearsed the Lord's summary of God's law for His creatures, the dual commandment of love, entire, unselfish love "with all our heart and soul and mind." It was a declaration of God's will and purpose for all His children. In the face of it, all men who come before His presence are judged. Thus in response all the people sang the *Kyrie:* "Lord, have mercy upon us"—that ancient cry of God's people throughout the centuries, whereby they acclaim His Lordship over them, admit their disobedience and failure to fulfil His law of love, and penitently seek again His pardon and aid.

With this brief, but searching and impressive preparation for true worship concluded, the celebrant and people mutually saluted one another, praying that the Lord be with them and their spirit as they sought His special revelation for them on this day. And the Collect for the day seemed to say to them all: "Stir up . . . bring forth plenteously the fruit of good works. Today is not the end, but a new beginning. Advent is at hand." So also in the Epistle, which the subdeacon read from the pulpit, the prophet Jeremiah's words pointed to the coming Kingdom of "the Lord our Righteousness," the consummation of all our work and labor, the gathering of all God's people from all nations and countries into unity and peace and "justice in the earth."

The revelation of such a glorious vision must evoke a response. It was a hymn of supplication for the dawn of this great Day:

> O Day of God, draw nigh
> In beauty and in power,
> Come with thy timeless judgments now
> To match our present hour.

Now the deacon was escorted to the pulpit to read the Gospel, the well-known story of the Feeding of the Mul-

PLATE XI

Free-standing Altar

(E. W. Hutchinson)

titude. What could be its lesson in this context? It is a story of hungry men and women, hungry for the bread that satisfies, bread that is not the source of contention and strife, but bread blessed and given with the blessing of Christ. It is a story of a small company of disciples without faith that their meager resources could be made sufficient for these hungry multitudes. But obedient to their Lord they gave Him all they had. Then they witnessed a great miracle. With the small offering of a lad, given freely and entirely, the Lord filled the multitude with such abundance that there was more left over than He had to begin with. This then was the revelation: if Christ's disciples would only let Him make their lives expendable, His Kingdom would come among us and all men would eat their bread in gladness and peace.

The faith of the Church in Him who "for us men and for our salvation came down from heaven" was recited by the congregation in St. Paul's with stronger conviction than ever. And they listened to the rector's sermon on the Gospel lesson with clearer insight into the meaning of this corporate act of Eucharist:

In that service we take bread and wine. What are these? They are the perfect symbol of the economic life of man. Before there can be bread the land must be ploughed, the seed scattered, the harvest gathered, the corn threshed, the flour baked; and before all that, there must be the gift of God in the life of the seed, the nurturing quality of the soil, sunshine and rain. Bread is an instance of God's gifts made available by human labour for the satisfaction of men's needs. The same is true of wine. In the production of these things, man co-operates with God. The farmer who cares for his land and neglects his prayers is, as a farmer, co-operating with God; and the farmer who says his prayers but neglects his land is failing, as a farmer, to co-operate with God. It is a great mistake to suppose that God is only, or even chiefly, concerned with religion. But of course the truly Christian farmer cares for land and prayers alike.

In the Holy Communion service we take bread and wine —man's industrial and commercial life in symbol—and offer it to God; because we have offered it to Him, He gives it back to us as the means of nurturing us, not in our animal nature only, but as agents of His purpose, limbs of a body responsive to His will; and as we receive it back from Him, we share it with one another in true fellowship. If we think of the service in this way, it is a perfect picture of what secular society ought to be; and a Christian civilization is one where the citizens seek to make their ordered life something of which that service is the symbol.[1]

After the sermon the rector returned to the altar to begin the Offertory. He chose one of the Offertory Sentences which seemed appropriate to the season and to the thoughts of the hour—thanksgiving, world mission, and the approaching Advent:

Jesus said unto them, "The harvest truly is plenteous, but the labourers are few: pray ye therefore the Lord of the harvest, that he send forth labourers into his harvest.

The choir repeated the anthem which they had sung on Thanksgiving Day, while the churchwardens received the money offerings of the people. Pledge-cards for the coming year were also placed on the almsbasin. While the gifts were being received, the crucifer and servers quietly moved down the side aisle of the church to meet the wardens and other representatives of the people— today they were a vestryman and one of the church

[1] William Temple, *The Hope of a New World* (New York: The Macmillan Co., 1941), pp. 69-70. By permission of the publishers.

school teachers—and escort them with their offerings up the center aisle to the sanctuary rail. The clergy met them there, the celebrant standing in the center, with the subdeacon on his right holding the breadbox which

PLATE XII

The Offertory

(A. J. Motelet)

had been on the sanctuary credence table, the deacon on his left carrying the paten and chalice.

The celebrant first received the alms and money offerings from the hands of the wardens and went up to present and place them on the altar. Then he returned to receive the oblations. The deacon held before him the paten on which he placed the breads presented first by the vestryman and next by the subdeacon. The other layman offered the cruets of wine and water with which the celebrant prepared the chalice. Then taking both paten and chalice from the hands of the deacon, the celebrant offered them and placed them on the altar, saying:

> Thine, O Lord, is the greatness, and the power, and the glory, and the victory, and the majesty: for all that is in the heaven and in the earth is thine; thine is the kingdom, O Lord, and thou art exalted as head above all.

Thus did the people make their offerings and prepare for the holy Sacrifice. When the celebrant said the Prayer for the Whole State of Christ's Church, they knew indeed that he was commending to God *our* oblations, and praying for the "truth, unity, and concord" of that "Universal Church" of which they were members and missioners. This noble prayer summed up the intention of the whole action in which they were engaged, the unity and love of all the members of the Body with their Head, Christ the Lord, to serve "in holiness and righteousness all the days of their life," until finally with all faithful servants they become "partakers of the heavenly kingdom."

All of them knew, however, that their offerings were the return to God of His gifts marked and soiled with the falsehoods, the disunity, and the discord of a selfish world and a divided Church. In penitence for their share of this "intolerable burden" they must confess their failings, and promise a fresh resolve "to lead a new life, following the commandments of God," before they dare to seek God's blessing and consecration of their gifts. So a General Confession was made by all, and the celebrant assured them of God's readiness to forgive and to strengthen them for all good work.

Now they could unite with joy and thanksgiving in

the great hymn of Consecration and lift up their hearts with faithful peoples "at all times and in all places" in the sacrifice of praise, the Church's "perpetual memory" of what the Lord Christ had wrought once for all to take away "the sins of the whole world." In the name of all the people the celebrant offered the holy gifts and creatures of bread and wine, that, being sanctified as Christ's Body and Blood, they might renew in all who partook of them Christ's life and entire self-giving in their own souls and bodies. With such strength and grace they could say with boldness the prayer the Saviour taught them: "Thy kingdom come. Thy will be done. . . ."

During the communion of the priest and his assistants in the sanctuary, the kneeling congregation joined the choir in singing one of the most ancient prayers of the Church, "Father, we thank thee . . .":

> Watch o'er thy Church, O Lord, in mercy,
>   Save it from evil, guard it still,
> Perfect it in thy love, unite it,
>   Cleansed and conformed unto thy will.
> As grain, once scatter'd on the hillsides,
>   Was in this broken bread made one.
> So from all lands thy Church be gather'd
>   Into thy kingdom by thy Son.

When the communion of all the offerers was finished, the celebrant said a brief prayer of thanksgiving for the spiritual food which they had received as "members incorporate in the mystical body" and for the grace to "do all such good works as thou hast prepared for us to walk in." To the thanksgiving of prayer all united to add the praise of the *Gloria in excelsis*. And the liturgy concluded with the Blessing of peace "which passeth all understanding." During the cleansing of the vessels and the return of the clergy and their servers to the sacristy the choir and congregation turned their thoughts and resolutions to the coming year of service as they sang the "Stir up" hymn:

Soldiers of Christ, arise,
 And put your armor on,
Strong in the strength which God supplies
 Thro' his eternal Son.

Stand then in his great might,
 With all his strength endued,
And take, to arm you for the fight,
 The panoply of God.

NOTES ON THE ILLUSTRATIONS

Consecrated in the year 1128, the present Basilica of San Clemente stands upon one of the oldest sites of Christian worship in Rome. Immediately beneath the church are the remains of a fourth century basilica; and at a lower level the original house-church, which dates from the first century, stands side-by-side with another building which enshrined a chapel of the pagan Mithra-cult. Tradition ascribes the ancient house to be the dwelling of St. Clement, the third bishop of Rome, and a disciple of the apostles. The chancel and pulpits, one on the Epistle side, the other on the Gospel side, are constructed from materials of the earlier basilica, and bear the monograms of Pope John II (532-35). The canopy or *ciborium* over the altar, and the Paschal candlestick (by the Gospel pulpit) are of the thirteenth century. There are few churches extant today that exhibit so perfectly as San Clemente the interior arrangements for worship in the basilicas built after the peace of the Church under Constantine in the fourth century.

PLATE I. *The Eucharist, Catacomb of Callistus, Rome.*

The early Christians often represented the Eucharist, as in this third century fresco in one of the "sacrament" chapels of the Catacomb of Callistus, by a symbolic reference to our Lord's blessing of the loaves and fishes and His miraculous feeding of the multitude. Here the loaves and fishes lie upon a tripod *(delphica)*, commonly used in the early centuries as a dining table. Such tables, made of wood or of metal, may often have served as "altars" in the ancient house-churches. The figure on the left, dressed in a philosopher's mantle (the *pallium*), represents Christ in the act of consecrating the oblations. The female figure on the right, in girded tunicle and veil, is variously interpreted as a symbol of the Church or of the Christian soul. Her standing posture, with arms stretched upwards, was the customary position taken by the early Christians at prayer—a posture still assumed by many celebrants at the Eucharist. The technical name for such figures in early Christian painting is *Orans* ("one who is praying").

PLATE II. *Mosaic Pavement, Basilica of Theodore, Aquileia.*

Underneath the present medieval basilica at Aquileia there was discovered a generation ago the remains of an early fourth century church built by one Bishop Theodore. It was a rectangular hall, about 130 feet long, divided into four sections by three pair of pillars. The entire pavement was covered with mosaic patterns, some of geometrical designs, others framing pictures of men and animals and the fruits of the earth. The eastern quarter of the basilica, the *presbyterium* where the clergy sat, is entirely given over to an aquarium scene, in which is depicted the story of Jonah. Near the center of this quadrangle is the dedicatory inscription of Bishop Theodore, placed probably just in front of his chair from which he presided over the Eucharist.

The two sections of mosaic presented in this Plate are located in the center of the quadrangle immediately adjoining the *presbyterium*. In the upper picture one may still see the marks of the legs of the holy Table that stood in this place. The mosaic of this square portrays a winged Victory, holding in her left hand a palm, and in her right, a crown. At either side are large baskets containing the breads of the Eucharist. This scene is unique in early Christian art. In the lower picture are to be seen the decorative motif of birds, and two offerers, one with clusters of grapes, another with a basket of bread. These undoubtedly represent the members of the Church with their oblations for the Eucharist and for the Church's charity to the poor.

PLATE III. *Old Testament Types of the Eucharist, Basilica of S. Apollinare in Classe, Ravenna.*

This magnificent basilica was consecrated in 549, but the mosaics of the lateral walls of the apse, of which this is one, are of the seventh century. In the center, behind the altar, is Melchizedek vested as an Oriental king. He is breaking one of the Eucharistic breads—two others lie on the altar with the chalice. To the left is

Abel offering a lamb, and to the right, Abraham is offering his son Isaac. Both Isaac and the lamb are symbols of Christ. The offerings of Melchizedek, Abel, and Abraham were considered in the ancient Church as types of the Eucharist, and they are referred to in the Canon of the Roman Mass as such. Note that the altar is five-legged, and that the linen altar cloth is embroidered with decorative designs. The two-handle chalice is a common form of the cup in this period.

PLATE IV. *Communion of the Apostles, Silver Paten from Riha on the Orontes, Syria.* (Dumbarton Oaks Research Library and Collection, Harvard University.)

The scene of our Lord administering Communion to His apostles, portrayed on this sixth century silver paten from Riha (near Antioch) in Syria, shows how the people at that time communicated. On the left an apostle with outstretched hands—his right hand placed on top of his left—receives the Bread. On the right another apostle, also with outstretched hands, drinks from the Chalice. The cloth he holds is designed to prevent any drops of the sacred Wine spilling to the floor. On the draped altar are another chalice and a paten with breads. The two objects between the chalice and paten are probably pieces of bread, oblations of the people, made in such a form in order to facilitate the breaking of the bread. The two columns with their architrave may represent either the screen dividing the chancel from the nave, or the ciborium about the altar. At the bottom of the paten are two vessels, a long-handled cup and a flagon. Their exact purpose in connection with the liturgy is not clear. Around the edge of the paten is a memorial inscription: "For the repose of Sergia, daughter of John, and for that of Theodosius; also for the salvation of Megalos, Nonnos, and their children."

PLATE V. *The Celebration of the Mass, Psalter of King Alfonso V of Aragon*, 1442. (British Museum MS. Add. 28962.)

This splendid miniature is a fine example of the costly, illuminated devotional books used by the wealthier laity in the late Middle Ages. The scene here depicted is a pontifical High Mass in the presence of the King and Queen and a congregation of monks and layfolk. The bishop, in chasuble and mitre, celebrates at an altar vested in embroidered frontal and white linen cloth. On the altar are the chalice and paten and one candle. Behind the altar is a handsome reredos with a statue of the Virgin and Child. Riddle curtains enclose the sides of the altar. Directly behind the celebrant stand the deacon and subdeacon, vested respectively in dalmatic and tunicle. The King and Queen are provided with prayer desks on which are placed their books of devotion. At the left a group of clerks gathered about a lectern chant the propers of the Mass—Introit, Gradual, etc.

PLATE VI. *The Canon of the Mass, The Tiptoft Missal*, 14th century. (The Pierpont Morgan Library, MS. 107.)

The page here reproduced gives the Canon of Consecration of the Mass, according to the Use of Sarum. The usages of the Church of Sarum (or Salisbury) were widely adopted in England in the late Middle Ages, and formed the basis for Archbishop's Cranmer's revision of the liturgy in the First Prayer Book of 1549. At the upper left corner the customary miniature of the Crucifixion, found in all Missals at the beginning of the Canon, is embellished with a scene of the elevation of the Host. This ceremony took place at the Words of Institution in the Canon. Behind the priest are the deacon and subdeacon in their customary vestments. Note that the subdeacon holds a veiled paten, since the paten did not rest on the altar during the Consecration in the Sarum usage. On the altar itself is a chalice and a folded corporal. The figures in the right margin of the page are St. John the Evangelist and St. John the Baptist. This manuscript was written in England before 1332, possibly in East Anglia.

PLATE VII. *Divine Service, St. Margaret's, Westminster*, early 18th century.

This engraving is from Ferdinando Warner's *An Illustration of the Book of Common-Prayer* (London, 1754). The parish church of St. Margaret, on the north side of Westminster Abbey, was founded in the eleventh century; but the present building, in the Perpendicular style of Gothic, was erected in the fifteenth century. St. Margaret's is the official church of the House of Commons. The engraving shows a typical seventeenth-eighteenth century arrangement for worship in a medieval English edifice. The altar stands against the east wall of the chancel, beneath the tablets with the Ten Commandments. It is vested in an embroidered carpet and enclosed by a rail. On it stand two Prayer Books. Directly in front of the great pulpit are the stalls for the rector and clerk, in a kind of three-decker arrangement. Opposite the pulpit is the pew of the Speaker of the House of Commons. The minister, vested in surplice, is reading one of the

Opening Sentences of Morning Prayer from the English Prayer Book.

PLATE VIII. *Holy Communion*, late 17th century.

This engraving serves as the frontispiece of Nathaniel Crouch's *Divine Banquet* (London, 1696), and portrays a characteristic sanctuary arrangement of an English church of the late seventeenth century. The tablets with the Commandments, required by the Canons of 1604, serve as a kind of reredos to the holy Table. On the altar are two loaves, a chalice, and two flagons, and at the north side a cushion with Prayer Book. The celebrant wears a surplice. His kneeling posture suggests that he is leading the people either in the General Confession or the Prayer of Humble Access.

PLATE IX. *Interior, Trinity Church, Newport, Rhode Island.*

Trinity Church is one of the finest examples of Georgian church architecture in America. Built in 1725, and later enlarged, it is the only church in America that still preserves a common eighteenth century arrangement, whereby the pulpit stands in front of the holy Table. However, the view of the Table is not hidden from the box pews. The wineglass pulpit was originally a two-decker, but the later addition of the clerk's stall below the reading desk has transformed it into a three-decker. The candles and the cross are, of course, more modern ornaments; but the tablets with the Commandments, Creed, and Lord's Prayer are part of the customary adornment of colonial times. There are galleries on three sides. In the back gallery (not shown in this picture) is the organ given to the parish by Bishop Berkeley, the eminent philosopher. It is surmounted by the crown of England and the bishop's mitre. The curved chancel with its large window is very similar to the plan of Christ Church (the Old North) in Boston.

PLATE X. *Holy Communion*, early 19th century.

This engraving is one of several that adorns an edition of the American Prayer Book, published in New York in 1827. The priest wears a large, flowing surplice and a black scarf. The scarf was not always worn by the clergy of this period. Note the shape of the paten, with its handle-base.

PLATE XI. *Free-standing Altar.*

Here the altar is free-standing, i.e., detached from the wall of the sanctuary. The priest is thereby enabled to stand behind the altar and face the people during the Eucharistic celebration. This was the universal custom in the ancient Church, and it is being widely adopted again in modern church design.

PLATE XII. *The Offertory.*

Another ancient custom, being revived in recent times, is the Offertory procession, wherein representatives of the congregation bring to the sanctuary not only the money offerings of the people, but also the bread and wine for the Eucharist. After the alms are presented at the altar, the oblations of bread and wine are then prepared before the people and offered at the altar. In this picture a deacon has just received the offering which he will give to the priest at the altar, and then return to the altar rail to receive the elements for the Eucharist.

BOOKS FOR
REFERENCE AND STUDY

Readers of the foregoing pages may find further information about the Church's services in the periods described, and also material on the life and work of the Church which formed their background, in the following works of reference:

CHAPTER I. Descriptions of the second century Eucharist are given us by St. Justin Martyr (*ca.* 150) in his first *Apology*, 65-67, translated by T. B. Falls, *The Writings of Saint Justin Martyr* (New York: Fathers of the Church, 1948); and by St. Hippolytus (*ca.* 200) in his *Apostolic Tradition*, translated with notes by B. S. Easton (Hamden, Conn.: Archon Books, 1962). For modern studies, see H. Lietzmann, *The Founding of the Church Universal* (New York: Scribners, 1950), pp. 124-47; and G. Dix, *The Shape of the Liturgy* (Westminster: Dacre Press, 1945), pp. 103-155. For the archaeological materials, see Michael Gough, *The Early Christians* (New York: Praeger, 1961).

CHAPTER II. English translations of the texts of the Latin liturgies of the sixth-seventh centuries are provided in R. C. West, *Western Liturgies* (London: S. P. C. K., 1938). A detailed description of the Roman liturgy and its celebration during this period is the *Ordo Romanus Primus*, translated with introduction and notes by E. G. C. F. Atchley (London: Alex. Moore, Ltd., 1905). Modern discussions may be found in J. A. Jungmann, *The Early Liturgy to the Time of Gregory the Great* (Notre Dame, Ind.: University of Notre Dame Press, 1959); and W. H. Frere, *The Principles of Religious Ceremonial* (New edition; London: Mowbray, 1928), pp. 59-74. Gough's book cited under Chapter I is also excellent for the archaeological background of the period. See also J. G. Davies, *The Origin and Development of Early Christian Architecture* (New York: Philosophical Library, 1953). Interesting applications of the liturgy in this period to the Prayer Book rite may be found in Walter Lowrie, *The Lord's Supper and the Liturgy* (New York: Longmans, 1943).

CHAPTER III. The liturgy described in this chapter is drawn from *The Sarum Missal in English*, translated by F. E. Warren (2 vols.; London: Mowbray, 1913). Vernacular devotions are taken from *The Lay Folks Mass Book*, edited for the Early English Text Society by T. F. Simmons (London: N. Trübner and Co., 1889). One should also consult *The Rationale of Ceremonial*, edited by C. S. Cobb for the Alcuin Club (London: Longmans, 1910). Much information is given in E. L. Cutts, *Parish Priests and Their People in the Middle Ages in England* (London: S. P. C. K., 1898); and F. A. Gasquet, *Parish Life in Mediaeval England* (3d edition; London: Methuen, 1909). An excellent summary is provided by J. R. H. Moorman, *Church Life in England in the Thir-

teenth Century (Cambridge University Press, 1945), pp. 68-89. For details of architecture, furnishing and decoration, see J. C. Cox and C. B. Ford, *The Parish Churches of England* (New York: Scribners, 1937).

CHAPTER IV. A useful commentary on the English Prayer Book of 1662 is that of Charles Wheatly, *A Rational Illustration of the Book of Common Prayer*, first published in London in 1710; a convenient edition is that of the Bohn Library (London, 1850). A good introduction to sources on liturgy in this period is G. W. O. Addleshaw, *The High Church Tradition* (London: Faber and Faber, 1941). Many details are given in J. W. Legg, *English Church Life from the Restoration to the Tractarian Movement* (London: Longmans, 1914). Of particular interest for the architectural background is G. W. O. Addleshaw and F. Etchells, *The Architectural Setting of Anglican Worship* (London: Faber and Faber, 1948). For a corresponding survey of American churches of the period, see S. P. Dorsey, *Early English Churches in America 1607-1807* (New York: Oxford University Press, 1952). The sermon in this chapter is drawn from Jeremy Taylor's *The Worthy Communicant* (1660).

CHAPTER V. Some interesting notes on the usages of the American Church are contained in Bishop John Henry Hobart's *A Companion for the Book of Common Prayer* (New York, 1805); the same author's *A Companion to the Altar* (New York, 1804) is drawn upon for the sermon in this chapter. Another excellent source is the *Reminiscences* of Bishop Thomas M. Clark of Rhode Island (New York: Thomas Whittaker, 1895), pp. 40-45. A summary account is given in W. W. Manross, *The Episcopal Church in the United States 1800-*

1840 (Columbia University Press, 1938), pp. 155-179. There are also materials in E. C. Chorley, *Men and Movements in the American Episcopal Church* (New York: Scribners, 1946).

CHAPTER VI. Basic for this chapter are the two works by A. G. Hebert, *Liturgy and Society* (London: Faber and Faber, 1935), and *The Parish Communion* (London: S. P. C. K., 1937). Descriptions are given in *Sunday Morning, The New Way*, edited by Brother Edward (London: S. P. C. K., 1938), and more recently by Basil Minchin in *Outward and Visible* (London: Darton, Longman and Todd, 1961). Suggestions and interpretations will be found in W. P. Ladd, *Prayer Book Interleaves* (New York: The Seabury Press, 1957), and a companion volume by M. H. Shepherd, Jr., *The Living Liturgy* (New York: Oxford University Press, 1946). See also the latter's *The Worship of the Church* (New York: The Seabury Press, 1952), and J. G. Davies, G. Cope, and D. A. Tytler, *An Experimental Liturgy* ("Ecumenical Studies in Worship," No. 3; Richmond: John Knox Press, 1958). The sermon in this chapter is taken from William Temple, *The Hope of a New World* (New York: Macmillan, 1941), pp. 69-70, by kind permission of the publishers.